MW00717319

Beyond Calliope's Garden
—poems of loss, love, and life—

Compiled by

Andrew Garrison

Edited by

Cassandra Drake

ISBN: 978-0-578-65495-9

Cover illustration © Jen Knanishu
Book design by Doris Tomaselli, Empress Creative
www.empresscreative.com
Printed by CreateSpace, an Amazon.com Company

Dedication

There are many people worthy of dedicating this anthology of poetry to, but one person stands out. I wish to dedicate this work to John James Sargent. John was a wonderful writer, a passionate fan of horror and science fiction—but most importantly he was a great friend. He was to be part of this incredible collection, but sadly he passed away before being able to finish his contribution. The years of friendship we shared will be something I will never forget. I thank him for all he taught me and all the support through that time. He may be gone, but his influence on my life will never be forgotten.

Special Thanks

I want to personally thank all the talented individuals who provided their poems for this collection. I am so proud to work with all of you and I'm excited to share these great works with the general public.

I want to thank Cassandra Drake, not only is she an incredible editor, but a talented writer as well. I wish to thank Jen Knanishu for the beautiful cover art. Of course, I can't forget Doris at Empress Creative for all her work behind the scenes of this and every anthology I've created.

Finally, I want to thank each and every one of you who has purchased this book or has shared it with others. The creative process is challenging, but few things are more difficult than spreading the word. We are eternally grateful for all that you have given us and we hope you enjoy the poems within.

Table of Contents

Heading Out

By James R. Scrimgeour

We are all packed, all ready to
go to the ocean, the state park
we visit every summer, when
we look up at the right moment —

wow — the incredibly bright
sun-lit leaves of the neighbor's
tree — the special lemon-lime
color of spring fills and fulfills

our vision; we can see nothing else,
not the thin dark branching limbs,
nor the bright blue, the perfect
blue background — we have not

yet seen the photo, we see only
the tree turned on, the miracle
of life exploding in small leaf
sized bursts — hard to imagine,

we think, climbing into our car,
hard to imagine anything more
beautiful than this — would be
nice if we could pack it in

our trunk, if we could keep
this small piece of spring
within us forever, no matter
where or when we go.

Buttercups, 2017

By James R. Scrimgeour

different this year I am in the middle
of what could be a thousand points of light,
Buttercup Village, see East Buttercup, there

to my right, isolated, living proud, off by
itself in a slightly higher elevation
and the inhabitants of West Buttercup

there to my left cavorting with immigrant
dandelions — see them playing, native
and immigrant in the midst of their too

short life span — each of the individual
windows glowing from the light within —
native and immigrant tipping their quaint

yellow caps to one another, nodding
hello, good-by in the fresh spring breeze.

Cardiac Dementia and the Tree
By James R. Scrimgeour

the one with the four limbs twisting,
sprouting so randomly, so unpredictably
from the single base, the tree, before which,

a mere three years ago, my friend Peter sat
gazing, writing a poem, a pretty good poem,
which I helped transcribe into his computer —

and I think of Peter the next year sitting
before the same tree looking at me with
that blank face when I ask him about

the poem, and today, me gazing at
the same tree thinking of the specialist:
"Cardiac Dementia, not Alzheimer's,"

he said, "He doesn't fit into our study.
It's irreversible! There's nothing we
can do for him." So each year he

remembers less and less, and yet
I think — so what — he really doesn't
need to remember — he lived it!

I've still got the poem,
and you've got this one.

Kitchen

By Mick Theebs

Home is where the heart is
and the heart is where the food is, or
more accurately, where food is
prepared and eaten.
Even in the most
unappetizing places
with puke green walls or
awkward salvaged furniture
built from junk and driftwood
splattered with splotches of
bile yellow pain,
even when it as warm and welcoming
as a steel bear trap
with dagger teeth ready to
snap into an unsuspecting ankle,
if there is food to eat
and a table to sit
it is home.

Witness

By Mick Theebs

I bet you didn't know
I was watching you
as you stalked the sidewalk
with that paper bag clutched in your hand
as if it had your very heart inside it.
I watched as
you tiptoed toward
a man sleeping on a park bench–
rail thin and dirty.
You left the bag next to his head
(he had no pillow to leave it under)
and then scurried off
looking over your shoulder only once
as the man stirred at the smell of
your heart in that bag.
I bet you thought
that no one knew.
But I saw you.
I saw you.

It's Only Water

By Mick Theebs

There will be a time
someday
soon
where you will be
lying drenched in sweat
parched tongue swollen
in the bottom of your mouth
like a slab of jerky
and you will think back to
every last drop of water
haphazardly spilled
on the floor or counter
and mopped up while
saying to yourself
with gratitude
"It's only water"
and you will want to laugh
and will not have the strength
and you will want to weep
and will not have the strength
and besides that
tears will be a waste
of that precious thing
that you once had
the privilege of squandering.

Sphinx

By Mick Theebs

She smiles,
though it transmits
no joy.

Rather, it is
a statement of
patience.

Her gaze is hungry,
but she does not have
bedroom eyes.

There is something in there
as she waits
in a silence
as hard as limestone
while you try
to answer her question,
that question
that has no answer.

Better men than you
have failed.

She does not
suffer fools
readily.

In a blink,
she will show her
strength.

continued...

Beyond Calliope's Garden

A flash of teeth,
a glint of claw.

A single motion
swift and deadly.

If by some miracle
you stumble on the truth,
she will make you king.

But she will never
belong to you.

Postmodern/Sublime

By Mick Theebs

They will hate me for this
I can't help it,
but my mother always told me that
honesty is the best policy even though
time and time and time and time again
this has been demonstrably false.
We have lost our way.
In our swirling maelstrom
of thoughts and impulses,
under the air raid siren
of mass media jamming its
fingers up our nostrils and
shoving a funnel down our throats
as we fumble like fools for
those special sunglasses that let us see
what's really written on the billboards
and finally read that
message behind the message,
we have totally and completely
lost the path, thread, compass, chart,
and also have no bars so
we can't even ask Siri to take us home.
We have turned to
considering consideration and
thinking about thinking
instead of ...thinking.
We do not build
to celebrate beauty or grace or
that special sauce that
makes everything extra spicy.

continued...

Beyond Calliope's Garden

Instead, we build
to deconstruct and
build to celebrate
the act of building
and stroke our chins
and tilt our heads
and give a quiet sage hum as if
that were at all the same thing as
admiring that sublime pulse
that throbs and courses through
every
miserable
goddamn
atom
of this place.
Instead we build shrines memorializing
The thoughts about that atom
and place frames around
the empty spaces where
frames once hung.
Meanwhile,
we bleed and burn and live
and die and fuck and dance
and drink and sing and play
and have dreams hopes fears
concerns about the growing police state
that go unheard unnoticed unwritten unread
because we are much too busy with
stupid bullshit questions that
gum up the works and
lock up the gears and
freeze you with
panicked analysis like

a child in front of Baskin-Robin's famous
32 flavors as you frantically try
to decide which one
you will have for dessert because
your father said
you may only choose one.
Of course there are some
That still carry the torch
through the long cold night
just dying for some relief
and if we don't do something soon
they're gonna drop from exhaustion.
So clear your minds
and wipe your eyes clean
of that sleepy sand that
makes you dream about dreaming.
Take in the beauty that is
all around you.
All you have to do is
pull your head out from
your navel and
look around.
Look around.
Look around.

Beyond Calliope's Garden

For Laura, April 2018.
By Joseph DeVellis

next time the power goes out,
let's be gods
who live up near the candle stars

and wield plastic bottles
filled with mighty catastrophes
to keep our double-a servants in check!

we'll watch the world die
with the return
of the great light;

mourning our dream silently
as we lay close together,
listening to the other breathe.

For Nancy, June 2018.

By Joseph DeVellis

her letter was less than a page long
but hopeful in its slanted cursive
as it wandered through the post office.

desperation passed between
an unaccountable amount of hands
until it fell down the wrong chute

and melted into a pulpy paste
under the fluorescent lights
that lorded over the basement.

every mailman wanted to feel guilty
when they heard its lopsided cries,
but couldn't find time to pause.

so everyone pretended not to notice
as they continued skimming names
and never saying hello to each other.

Beyond Calliope's Garden

For Jerusha, May 2018.
By Joseph DeVellis

he vowed to chain my wrists up
after i awoke
too early for his liking.

i laid there
bearing a vacant frown,
aroused by no apparent feeling

but perhaps
the insipid refusal
to reclaim my childhood?

i lolled in the courtyard afterward
and let the summer gods
bless my skin

with pollen,
ticks,
and the reds of flowers.

For Corey, March 2018.
By Joseph DeVellis

true happiness
snuffed out her cigarette
and scoffed.

"what an accusation
against this fundamental part
of existence!

once again,
you're remarkably wrong
about why people do what they do.

listen:
don't even call it love.
such specificity is meaningless.

just become aware
of those you care about
on a physical level."

For Ken, June 2018.

By Joseph DeVellis

he took an ornate mirror to his scalp
and inspected each
of his delicate hairs

for any insidious strays
that made it past the years
of mousse and careful abuse.

but every follicle yielded to his neuroticism,
finding their own definition of servitude
as they let the man be his own undoing.

Love Is Not a Day

By Andrew Garrison

It may blossom
Like a spring wildflower
But it matures slowly

Like a mighty redwood.
Planting roots far and deep
Climbing to majestic heights.

The foolish seek to control it
And the cruel to break it
No chains will fetter love
Free-flowing as energy

It has no weapons of war
But it possesses great power.
Love like water against stone

In time, it carves its own path.
For love is not a day
it is a gift.

Snowlight

By Andrew Garrison

Snowflakes descend upon a quiet New England town
A scarred winter landscape layered with pillow-soft snow
Beautiful in its purity, yet cruel in its indifference
Unyielding, stunning, a force through the eons.
Upon its smooth surface, shadows creep through the night.
Crossing fields and sprawling throughout forests.
They move in silence, a gift in deafening times.
Revealing a quietude long forgotten
Except for those brave souls who stare out
to accept, to wonder, to embrace,
the simple kindness
of a snowfall upon a silent winter night.

Sour Liberty

By Andrew Garrison

Give me your tired, your poor, your forlorn
Bring me your huddled masses longing to be free.
For I shall cleanse them.

My words once true
Now fall upon deaf ears.
Betrayed by the corrupted
Feeding blind, unwitting masses
the filth of rage, hate, and fear

Once I was a gift from an ally
A beacon of freedom, hope, and prosperity
Now I'm a rusting relic of a bygone age

I am not an icon of this new America,
For this country grows ever dimmer
and my lamplight has been extinguished.

Luna

By Andrew Garrison

Silver Luna glimmers in purple sky
Beckoning to the dreamers
To play in her subtle glow

In borrowed light
She roams
Solitary and celestial
Scarred, yet beautiful.

To light our way
Through the shadows
Until new dawn.

Portuguese: Da noite

De Bruno dos Santos Silva

Certamente a noite é mais viva. O dia apenas goza dessa aparência, mas é a noite que realmente detém esse privilégio. À noite os sentidos aguçam-se, a mente expande-se, os fantasmas atormentam-nos, as regras revogam-se, os desejos libertam-se, as fantasias realizam-se e a presa torna-se mais vulnerável. A noite é o momento do prazer, do medo e do espetáculo. Um brinde a cada ocaso!

English: Of the Night

By Bruno dos Santos Silva

Certainly the night is more alive. The day only enjoys that appearance, but it is the night that really holds that privilege. At night the senses are sharpened, the mind expands, the ghosts torment us, the rules are revoked, the desires are released, the fantasies are realized and the prey becomes more vulnerable. Night is the moment of pleasure, of fear and of spectacle. A toast to every sunset!

Portuguse: As dores

De Bruno dos Santos Silva

Toda dor é a mais dolorida: a dor do insulto, a dor da re-
jeição, a dor do fracasso, a dor do medo, a dor do excesso, a
dor da falta. Nosso alívio é que sofremos de várias maneiras,
e uma dor embota a outra, talvez por isso a persigamos. A
dor é nossa memória. A dor é nossa redenção.

English: The Pain

By Bruno dos Santos Silva

All pain is the most painful: pain of insult, pain of rejection,
pain of failure, pain of fear, pain of excess, pain of failure.
Our relief is that we suffer in many ways, and one pain dulls
the other, perhaps that is why we pursue it. Pain is our mem-
ory. Pain is our redemption.

Hindsight

by Cassandra Drake

Sometimes love is fleeting
Sometimes love endures
Sometimes a chance meeting
Does little to assure
That when the morning light
Awakes us from our sleep
The magic from that night
Is something we could keep
Will I want to know your fears
And will you ask me mine
Will you wipe away my tears
And say I will be fine
Will we take the good and bad
As together we grow old
Or will I want what I could have had
As half my bed grows cold

Undercover
by Cassandra Drake

You came in with a warm winter wind
Sweet and salty from the swirling ocean air
Shivers whispering along my skin
Dreams of a future lived without a care

I could see it clear as day
Us walking the shore hand-in-hand
Laughing at the things you'd say
Secrets only we would understand

We'd leave footprints in the sand
Soon to be washed away by the tide
I'd ignore that golden band
And you would ignore mine

We'd collect shells and feathers
Bottle up sand to remember as we grow old
A keepsake of our first December together
Before that warm winter wind turned cold

When that first snowflake fell
And that water was too cold for our toes
We'd seek refuge in that same hotel
Where we met those days ago

I'd relish the feel of your skin on mine
You'd trace each curve of my face
We'd spend a lazy morning
Wrapped in a tight embrace

But soon the alarm bell would ring
And our time would come to a close
You'd promise me any and everything
No matter what happened I should know

That you'd be back for me next year
When the warm weather turned cool
Even I knew that summer was for lovers
And winter was for fools

A Hellish Perfection

by Cassandra Drake

An image spun through my mind
Her face a treasure for me to find
Each breath she took I was consigned
Let our fates never entwine

Lost little lamb took a seat next to me
I couldn't move I couldn't breathe
She smelled so sweet, of strawberries
Her skin a saccharine delicacy

Perfectly still she sat, resigned
Every move she made stuck in time
Repeating constantly as if by design
Foolishly her beauty turned me blind

Each glance I steal I do so secretly
Chase her away before she finally sees
The truth I have buried down deep beneath
I will always know this misery

Only devils can balance such duplicity
Now I must regretfully leave perfection be.

Heartsease Κίρκη

By Benjamin Kissell

Shades of wine
      [for have we not always called it the wine-dark sea?]
intersect with deepest blues and ugly bruises of violet and saffron
      [treacherous as that tri-coloured blossom of Cupidean repute]
and they gambol about the shimmering reflection of my Father
Helios, far below his blazing chariot, as he passes Grandfather
Oceanus towards loving Nyx' dark embrace.
A warm draught tugs at me as brazen light plays upon the waves
where they cross
      [ever dancing, never stopping, always calling the Anemoi to
      the Pelagos]
slowly closer and ever farther of the shore.
Aeaea.
To see the island is to rejoice.
To see the sky is to know freedom.
To feel the breeze
      [is that a kiss from flitting Zephyrus or was it his headstrong
      brother, Boreas?]
is to love.
To remember ... ahh, that is to ... what was the word that half-mad
sailor used?
Ah.
Yes.
To remember is to 'crack'.
And so I crack.
Thunderously silent.
Ætna and Thera shook their foundations with less force than this (for
all their memorable qualities) and my world's foundation is sundered
for a moment.
Memories trickle about me, falling/fleeing/flying, from the cataclysm

continued...

that is my heart.

They fall, crystalline, about as adamant pearls strewn to the lawns
and pebble'd beach – to the portico'd halls and rough cliff walls
    [beautiful and terrible]
and I stoop to gather every one of them to my breast.

[If you could make someone love you, would you; by herb or grass,
by bloom or sacred moly?]

The fires of Cyclopean forges never dared to burn so hot as the
passions of an immortal's heart, nor do their blackened cinders
    [cold and fragile, these broken fragments]
floating upon the breeze, lost to night, bear proof of our faults less.

    [They say no one's heart was ever more susceptible than
    Hers; Why? No one knows. It may be that the cause lay in
    Her very nature]

Mortals love and pass into wind, embraced and darkened by
Grandmother Earth, seeking the release of Lethe; but immortals?
We love and play at love more truly, more fiercely, more terrifyingly
than any monster born of man for we cannot forget – no matter how
we shatter our selves in the attempt.

    [the greed and curse of my brother-in-law's love and hubris
    stalked the halls and corridors of his Daedalus-built labyrinth]

A heart, once broken – spurned for the sake of another – is not
balmed by liquor of love-in-idleness nor cured by Dian's bud.

    ["Leaves will grow on the sea, and sea-weed flourish on the
    mountain-tops before I change my love," he cried]

Tho' we, gods or men, do try our best to assuage it; to hinder it
with companions – willing or no, still it gnaws with carrion beaks at
our hollow ribs. With Cypress pine, bough and root, I pulled them to
me; to purr, to whinge, to growl, to comport themselves with animal
glee in affection for my greatness. For my own love to seek.

    ["Not you, but Scylla – who would change a 'falcon' for
    a dove?"]

For, I could not have his.

Never his.

No matter the man or god whom I felt my own immortal heart
drawn to – be he wanderer or fish-scaled mourner – nursing his own
scorned or wounded heart he would not truly turn his towards me.

> [Offended/hurt/broken, She crushed together such herbs
> whose juices had a power, and, singing spells She had learned
> from Triple-named Hecate, She mixed them.]

And being a jealous goddess, I ...

I ...

I crack again, more diamonds fall from my eyes as my breast
heaves and the beech trees about me sway in an aetherical storm of
thought and pain and memory.

> [Then She put on a robe of sky and left her palace-halls,
> through beasts that fawned around her, and over the boiling
> tide She sped, dry-shod as if on solid ground, to a particular
> pool. And She dyed this pool with bitter poisons]

About me, I hear the cries of beast and fowl, alarum and fright.
And I shall sing to them, my children and my loves, that they shall
hear that I am not afraid – nor should they be.

> [She poured liquids brewed from evil roots, and murmured,
> with lips well-skilled in magic, and thrice nine times, a charm
> obscure with labyrinthine language and there the nymph,
> beautiful Scylla came; wading into the waters.]

The Journeyman, wanderer, has left these shores – was it the first or
the last time? I've forgotten already – homeward bound; towards his
melancholy and his heart; towards his pain and his relief. So much
of the former to achieve the latter ... and none of it given for me.

> [Waist-deep, and suddenly saw her legs disfigured/changed/
> cursed with barking monsters; she could not believe that
> these were parts of her own body and she tried in vain to
> drive them off – these barking creatures. In fright, Scylla fled
> the waters but took them with her, for were they not now
> her? The heads of monstrous dogs, her thighs, jaws gaping

continued...

wide and mad, she was circled by these monstrous forms.
   And Glaucus, the silver-scaled god, wept at the sight and fled]
my embrace.
Too cruel, my heart, with potent herbs and spells and jealousy.

   [To vent her implacable hate, Scylla there fixed, upon Circe
   she robbed the wanderer, Odysseus Ulixes, of all his company
   she could in screams and pain]

I crack again and the storm thunders, the waves crash. It is more
than I deserve and no less than I have earned and yet ...
and yet.
I've gathered them to my arms – my bare arms glow 'neath the
stars – the crack'd pearls and adamant tears which fled me at the
onset; hearing a cry, I look to the heavens
   [flapping, flyting, fleeing, coming, roosting]
and spy brightly against the dark a falcon, my namesake/sigil/
consort. He has brought to me – a good fellow he was/is – such a
sprig of palest silver-green colour that I cannot help but fix upon it.
The gems I've gathered seem lighter now; lighter than Aeolus' kiss
and Father Helios' glance.
Are they gone? I cannot feel them.
I cannot feel ...
I ...
   [see as thou wast wont to see / be as thou wast wont to be]
I look around me, at my wonderful island, filled with animalia and
Animals who love me and I am content.
I have always been content, haven't I?
The green, dark 'neath this midsummer's moon-less night, is the
world at rest and a better bower I could not think of nor desire – the
lamplit palace halls do not call to me this even. No. The darkness is
where my heart does lead me
   [We follow darkness like a Dream]

Snippets of song remain flitting in my tresses, sung by men who were
never there and women who can only hear me in their dreams and
secret hopes.
The Children of Earth, of rock and sea and foam and sky, they
remember me
      [they love me still]
and they sing. But their songs are unheard, misunderstood and
ignored, by Man.
They sing to the Muses, to the Gods.
They call and I join them in the night-dark:

And now, O Muse Calliope – beloved daughter of Zeus, loved forever
in Dream and memory – sing to me of myself – of Aeaean Circe.
And a voice, forever and always knit within yet separate from even
one such as myself, answers my/their/our plea:

    In honeyed words
    She descends.
    Fire and rage and loss
    She torments.
    The Achaeans lost and found
    She regrets.
    Shap'd and twist'd in the moly
    She laments.
    Only one man
    Whose sails ragg'd and shorn
    From the Cyclops' wrath
    Had been borne
    From her bosom
    She revenges and is revenged upon.
    Heartsease is found.

And in the darkness, I cry happy tears.

Rose Colored Glasses Collection
By Morgan Marin

Poem #1:

In that midnight sky
I could feel the stars above me
they were never more beautiful
than in that moment.
I sat upon that dock
tracing the reflection of the moonlight
on the water
and for once
the dark wasn't so frightening.

Poem #2:

I hear the crashing waves,
every tide comes in,
as the ocean renews.
I lay in the sand
not minding the waves
they can take me
wherever they may be heading.
this salt water
I could swear it smells like a new life,
it's something more deep,
and it feels like,
out of my body
into the waves
is where these emotions seep.
I see the sailboats in the distance,

floating away from the shore
into the wind
how can I go with them?

Poem #3:

I lost myself among the fields
with every hill I had climbed
there is nothing that can compare
to the blinding sun
among us.
why when I am surrounded
by the most beautiful pieces of nature
do I find you
more appealing?

Poem #4:

I wish that the way we told stories
were not from memories
but from bringing us
to that place
and that time
and at once we can experience
all these beautiful things
ourselves.
we want those stories
in our hearts
and our minds
for our own
and when we share them

continued...

with the world
they could never truly know
without their presence in that memory.

Poem #5:

I want to feel alive
walking through the mountains
of New York
and touching the sky
in Alaska
just as the northern lights appear.
I want to breathe the humid air into my lungs
in Florida
and drive up the coast
of California
midday
as the sun is at its highest.
I want to dance on the shore
of the Fiji islands at dawn
and kiss alongside the Eiffel Tower.
because if I never do any of these things
have I ever really lived at all?

Poem #6:

Our souls are very lost
trying to search for the light
but what we didn't know
is that it's been there every night
when the sun finally sleeps

and the moon begins to wake.
we map out the rhythm of the sun
following it with every step
but we never considered
that the moon may be more worth
traveling along with.

Pleonasm

By C. Vincent DeVellis

Let go
of a hand
aching to float

and up there
you drift

weightless

maybe up there
you can find
a sometime
where you only cry from joy

Circadian
C. Vincent DeVellis

The easy morning sun seeing through the blinds
with sugar cane kisses
spilling all around my feet.

She's warm, the sun, smiling and
dancing and burning and spinning
through fields overgrown with tall,
painful fire-grasses, still drenched with the
dark rum falling from the deep blue
night sky.

Keeping the stars pinned up
      like butterflies on a board.

Keeping the fires burning
      gentle
            white
                  smoke
                        drifting into the distance.

After a time,
      it all dissipates.

Ballad to Skids

By Brian K. Thaler

My car...is awesome.
2002 4-door Hyundai Accent
accents of cheap silver plastic trim,
chipped paint.
Power locks? It ain't got 'em!
Man-u-al, all the away.
Clutch, windows, doors, locks,
constantly busted engine block.
Glock? No, damn it!
I'm from Culpeper,
we've got gun racks on our autos!
Well...I don't...
I've got leopard print seat covers,
Yankee candle air freshener
(homemade apple pie, yum)
camera tripod on the backseat,
fluffy slippers on the floor,
and a box of in-your-face bumper stickers
that I have yet to grow to appropriate sized balls
to slap on my rear bumper.
Nu-uh! No tonsil-hockey in my backseat, kiddos!
If anyone gets to defile the sanctity of
my mobile sanctuary,
it's gonna be me!
And that's not gonna happen anytime soon.
I'm never buying used again.
I name him Skids,
'cause that's what he did the first time I drove him.
Tried to drive him.
Drove him right over the yellow line,

no time to correct before screeching brakes
and it takes a full 30 seconds to pull us back over,
Dad's knuckles white as his
saucer-sized eyes yell before his voice can:
"Shift! Shift! SHIFT!"
"I'm trying!"
I've never driven stick before.
Good thing I live on a country road.
Skids is a he, 'cause he's an annoying little
5 gear ass who won't tell me what's wrong
until he's screaming it
in steel coated agony.
I lost my male-ginity to Skids,
awkward adventures in driving, shuddering,
shifting, stuttering starts and abrupt ends.
I hate hills.
I hate old people, who, above all other,
possess the innate ability to cruise at speeds
right in-between each of my gears.
Grinding gears.
Grinding MY gears.
Fearing more stall,
Crawling at snail paces where in other places
pedestrians move faster than us.
Stupid old people with the coupons and
exact change and unnaturally colored hair.
Old people with their bald heads and laser eye
surgery
And newfangled phones they barely know how to
use
That quack.
And the smell.
Old man Settle sold me the thing,

continued...

Beyond Calliope's Garden

One dent on the driver's side door,
Nicks on the roof,
Old man smell inside, free of charge.
Even after my Yankee apple buffer,
The smell blasts me whenever I use the AC.
Old man smell. Blegh.
I planned to go one morning.
On my way to work, just go.
Speed past the store and never look back.
Unload my bank account and never look back.
Leave everything, and never look back.
Sixteen-year-old brains use simple equations.
Car + me = freedom.
Years of experience teaches a new formula:
Car + me = variable of job + variable of insurance
+ variable of gas + variables unforeseen.
Leopard print pays the bills as well as
it can changes its spots.
Switch the sensors, repairs the pipes,
Every few months, even more maintenance
just to make it run right.
No time for childish fantastical flights,
no cash.
All of it went to replace the spark plugs,
quelling the squall beneath my scratched hood,
thunder reverberates through steering wheel columns
and grips
It's never fully fixed; it's all downhill from here.
I'm never buying used again.

Feet Along the Narrow Path

By Brian K. Thaler

smooth rocks, a river road's
slant flowing out with green.
tree trunks, sandbars,
ant villages hide unseen.
clinging dirt, rough steps,
leaf ferries twist and glide.
quick feet, rodent swift,
dens so deep and wide.
highway of moss, dandelions seeds,
the road less traveled is less bare.

The Gem in Two Eyes
By Mark Buder

One an angel,
The other a demon.
One with true love,
The other with anger.

They fell in love,
Forbidden love,
But true love.

They changed each other,
Made each other see.
The good in both,
Bad too.

Their love a secret,
Forced to stay in shadows.
But everyone knew...

Their love was so strong,
A force formed around them.
When they were together,
Everyone saw.

A kiss was forbidden,
Between the two.
If good kissed evil,
Cursed they shall be.

But they wanted to so much,
Care not about the curse.
So that night,
Lips collided.

And cursed they be,
Forced to share one life,
One body...

Gemini was born...

Love
By Mark Buder

Sometimes,
love is unpredictable,

We think,
In our mind,
How our loved one will look like.

We go out with people who
feed.....

That image.

Our reality,
Is quite the opposite.

Strong,
Dark,
Handsome.

Could be.....
Dorky,
Silly,
Weak.

Love come in many sizes.

Nor is love perfect.

But love keeps you.......
Thinking,
Wondering,
And hoping.

Romance,
Moments,
Are what comes from it.

Like a rose,
Stands for everything.

A Conversation with the Sky

By Michael A. Petrino Jr.

I look up at you frequently throughout the day
You mesmerize me with your colors
I appreciate our wordless conversations
While others may not like your tears
I sympathize with your thunderous cries
It's cleansing, powerful and romantic

To stand outside soaking, with my head held high
Your colors of pink, purple, blue, orange, and grey
are by far the best gift that you give to me

On this day I looked at you with admiration
Within your clouds arouse a sun of inspiration
Together forming a site filled with decoration
I whispered up to you my aspirations

You winked at me through the clouds
then I walked away into the day
With only one thing left to say...

Nice talk!

A Plea to My Siren

By Michael A. Petrino Jr.

The shame I feel, I cannot bear to look at your face. I hide
my eyes to not show you my tears. You long for me as I
do you in a lustful, sinful, desire, to feel the warmth of our
bodies together. Your plea for me resounds in my head
like that of the siren's song. Do let me go, let me think
for myself without first thinking of you. I need not to be
spellbound by your goddess-like features, but freed from the
absurdity that constantly has me at your wish. I want to
love you but know there is no love to be returned. I hate to
want you, knowing it is exactly what you want from me. I
exposed myself, the weakness of a man is as simple as the
beauty of a woman. Your trickery lured me in while your
witchery kept me blinded. I plead to you my Siren; do not
whisper in my ear, for your voice alone makes it impossible
to leave. Do not touch me any longer, as your warmth
wrongfully gives me nothing to fear. I ask of you my Siren,
if I am just a man to you, if there is no love to be had, let
these desires sink beneath the sea and blow away into the
wind, for I long to be loved and no longer to be desired.

Dracula's Daughter

By Michael A. Petrino Jr.

She comes with the wind.
Never knowing when she will appear
And just as unexpected she will disappear.

People fear her presence.
I am completely aware of her existence.
Loving her, I resent her choice of distance.

Her voice is spellbinding.
Her words spoken so alluring.
She has perfected the art of tempting.

Families have all felt her fear.
She has taken the ones we hold dear.
She leaves, yet makes me feel she's near.

My youngest of brothers was taken.
Jealousy fills my heart which is broken.
Wishing it was me she sank her teeth in.

I invite her with exposed veins.
Enticing her, knowing her bane.
In an attempt no less than vain.

The daughter of the Prince of Darkness.
Taking after a life of greatness.
Becoming her own Queen of Temptress.

Lust, I can't help but lust.
Emptiness fills the area beneath her bust.
If she saw a sunrise she would turn to dust.

Take me, take me, I plead.
Willing for her to make me bleed.
I know deep inside it is her I need.

Taunting and teasing, knowing I would be her slave.
I'll take this love for her straight to my grave.
Just like that she is gone with the wind.

Mindless Bit Of Wandering

By Michael A. Petrino Jr.

I took a stroll down to the sea
To clear my mind of everything
And stood beside a lonely tree.

The Winds were blowing steadily
The clouds above were emptying.
I took a stroll down to the sea.

Not knowing what was wrong with me,
I got lost in my wondering,
and stood beside a lonely tree.

Maybe, this would set my mind free.
This mindless bit of wandering.
I took a stroll down to the sea,
And stood beside a lonely tree.

The Empty Vase

By Michael A. Petrino Jr.

I stare at this vase all day long
It is empty, just like me.
It is everything that went wrong
And all that I couldn't see.
My love, such a sad song,
My love, where could you be.

I never meant for this to be
You have been gone too long,
All that resounds is our song.
The emptiness you left in me
If only you could see,
I know I did you wrong.

Being without you feels wrong,
I know we are meant to be
But what is it that you see
To keep you away this long?
Just please come back to me
So we can sing a different song.

Have you grown tired of our song?
All this time have I had you all wrong?
Were you ever in love with me?
Did you ever really want us to be?
I've been asking these questions too long,
I need you to be able to see.

continued...

Beyond Calliope's Garden

Everything we are you do not see.
The love we celebrate with song,
The love we shared for so long.
All this time can't be wrong.
What you wanted us to be
How you said you loved me.

Just tell me was it me?
Was there something I couldn't see?
Is there a chance for us to be?
Stop me from hearing that song,
The one that shows this is wrong.
I hate that I've loved you for so long.

One more time for me, will you sing our song?
So maybe you might see, how leaving was wrong.
Just know that I won't be, alive for too long.

Tonight We Go To Paradise

By Michael A. Petrino Jr.

Every night we dream together
Far apart in separate beds.
Tonight, different than any other
We dream lying side by side.
I'll hold you in my arms.
Rest your head on my chest.
I'll take you far away
We sleep tonight in Paradise.
Stay close, barely move
Make sure our bodies touch.
Don't open your eyes,
The night will never end.
Keep the lights off
Don't turn the alarm on.
We don't have to wake
Tonight we sleep in Paradise.
Just like every other night
This one will come to an end.
We don't have to let it,
We stay together in our hearts.
If you want to see me
Close your eyes and there I am.
Don't worry about tomorrow
Tonight we go to Paradise.

With a Wink

By Michael A. Petrino Jr.

I sat next to her
Looking across at you.
Your eyes never left me,
My eyes only on you.

She reached for my hand
And all I felt was you.
You smiled.
I fell in love.

I knew you were confused,
My mind was running wild.
I couldn't stop looking at you,
No one else mattered.

Without a word being spoken,
I winked and you knew,
Someday soon,
It would be me and you.

Obstacles

By Stephen Harris-Dixon

Turmoil takes the day and shapes it

The artist of life is messy, like a child

The glitter is everywhere; on my hands, in my clothes

Adorning me and making me laugh

My laugh is the will of the Elephant-headed God Ganesh

Removing obstacles is inner work

Rocks of the heart smashed with the hammer of mirth

Smile, and then some

Michael

By Stephen Harris-Dixon

The wind came to be, made of the palaces of mermaids and sea witches

Mother said to him, "Don't grow up so fast!"

Yet grow he did, big and strong and terrifying

Eating what warm food he could

He said to himself, "I will go to the seaside town!"

Michael was his name; he came without invitation

Just to huff and puff like that wolf that ate small pigs

The manatees stood at the gate and said, "No, you mustn't come in!"

Brutish, selfish, he would not listen

Michael crashed the party anyway, a bad non-guest

Like the waves that crashed against the shore

He broke the roof

Blew out the candles

Poisoned the well

The seaside city fell asleep for years to come

Until the kiss of the people's love could awaken it once more

Mother put Michael out after a time; death dressed him well

This is a thin blanket that does the job

But Mother cautions us that though Michael is gone

Mermaids and sea witches always build palaces

Halloween Tea

By Stephen Harris-Dixon

Grandmother put the kettle on for the annual Halloween tea

Pip, pop! Pip, pop! goes the steam, creating jack-o'-lantern puffs

"Tonight, we worship the Witches' Queen!" she said with a grin

And I couldn't help but giggle and chime in as the black cat rubbed against my legs and purred

"And Father-in-the-Earth, the Hunter, the Guardian, the Lord of Death!"

Grandmother's eyes twinkled with that sparkle only she could have

"Yes, yes, my child! We'll dance with the Dead and the Spirits of Night! Yes, yes, my child!"

Pip, pop! Pip, pop! goes the kettle for tea!

"We'll wear our black cloaks and tall hats and carry our broomsticks;

Whether storm or stars, we'll walk the paths of old and work our will by magic rite."

Grandmother set out the cups and the cookies and brought us the kettle

And she poured for me, and I poured for the cat, and the cat poured for her

Tea for three, tea for you, tea for me! A magical tea on old Halloween

When dark in the night we'll worship the Queen of Witches and Father-in-the-Earth

Pip, pop! Pip, pop! goes the steam of the kettle, and a voice whispers, "Happy Halloween, my child!"

continued...

Beyond Calliope's Garden

Tears in her eyes, Grandmother looks up to see who has come to greet her

Why, Great-Grandmother is here, without her fleshly costume, carrying her own ghostly kettle of tea

And she sits with us, completing our merry lot of magic

Her eyes sparkle, and then I know where Grandmother gets the twinkle in her eyes

One day, hopefully, my eyes will shimmer on Halloween

As I pour tea for daughter and granddaughter

New York City

By Keith Roland

Where glitter gods walk
Black hole eyes stalk
Feet by foot, street by block
Locking down dynamics
Lighting up little lanterns
Living life by night
Fight or flight anthems
Ringing limelight corridors
Stringing together raucous
Rousers fleet foot
Single soot shout outs
At karaoke bars
Bringing way out stars
Way back
Double mac burger attack
The pizza places open past midnight
Singing sleuths slinging shoes
Uncouth daycare at 2 am
Life ain't fair,
But here I am again.

Mixtape

By Keith Roland

I guess we'll leave pock marks
Like your first scars
Healed away but help to slay the stars
From the depths of puberty
Come you and me
Strengthened humanity
Willing to see the breaches
Impeach the heavy streets
Wearing on bones
Mr. Jones and me ain't got fairytales
Just walking wailing entities
Talking up deities and supersedes
Hoping for that goddamn Mercedes
Lingering back of parking lots
Counting up our bullets
Bulletin board best bought truth anthems
Singing about how alcohol could be
Our next best pastime

I wonder wonder
About how we blunder
Through best times and worst times
Still find the truth down under
The silken sheets
Cuz where we meet
Hasn't meant much to me
But how we act
Feeling up the back tracks
Of way way out kicked back
Starstruck half-assed

Fun to fuck with
But not to eat
Anthems

So swell the galaxies
Dilute them into reality
Let's just make it a mix
For you and me

My Sweetheart, The Forest Fire
By Drew Mazur

Until another lonely heart
Will take me even deeper
A shrine forever in her depths
A marrow I will feed her

The vines and weeds'll eat my soul
My brain will grow a new stem
I'll fall into her entrapments
And suffocate within them

This green mold will collect on me
And seep into my belly
And if she fails to kill me
In my narcissistic dwellings

I will stay here, pining
As I grow into the sky
She gathers bitter sap
In my golden, gooey eyes

And now the calm mentality
Is lost inside your haze
I am your greatest regret
I am the dying flame

The constellations on her shoes
I stole her greatest lie
With tantalizing radiance
A cancellation prize

I'm taking all her alibis
To recreate my fears
Another loss to flood me in
These wet, redundant tears

For if it had inspired me
I'd surely crisp by flame
She came on me like kerosene
And brushed the ash away

Jade

By Drew Mazur

no longer jaded / simply jade / converted in her image / in a forest of green / her dress was a chamber / of lush jade / a silhouette / reflects the beauty around her / point out Polaris to her / but it's a light on the bay of Peekskill / enveloped in her / a magician / everything we touch becomes magic / where heartbreak used to play / with the tangled weeds of heart / she's become a cataclysm / the sorceress of healing / a pink within the crystal / seasoning prosperity / an eternal firefly / as she flies away / into shadow

Eclipse
By Drew Mazur

In Manhattan we get lost among indie theatres, grind queens and outlet
windows, hipster Adonises and Persephones, Italian lovers and
Black heroes, neon thieves and purgatories as we amble away
from One World Trade Center

In Manhattan there is hope springing existential, expensive coffee,
gates that stand between Jersey and us
In Central Park we watch out over Belvedere Castle for an hour,
an eternity

In Manhattan we educate, deescalate, invigorate a viral Strand, satirical
literature with babble and genitals, great verse to bumfuzzle,
bleeding tongue hydrolysis, phonetics, tethering sensitive
magnetism

In Manhattan there are regnboga towers of beer, Hades' twilight,
serving us tequila and scotch; yellow yellow yellow

In Manhattan the sensual revolution is born, Washington Square Park,
NYU students retired, soft-lip Utopia, Kennedy jazz musicians,
bourbon, slowly finished espresso, receding fingers that
consoled, sax man in unison with the backing trucks, lost little
campus couples with campus rings

In Manhattan, a blood-red moon, lunar intermittent moments of
Megan's laughter, white shrouds and the joy moderates, the
majestic spotlight of Bryant Park, astronomy, astrology and
Aquarius philosophy; she doesn't like to quit

Rock Sculptures
By Drew Mazur

I am a Tuesday person – I drink sake
I write drunk and drink editing

Bias is how I spend my mornings
Infamy is how I sleep in the evening

there is no need for a cigarette
when you have pessimism up your sleeve

this is the social revolution – not the words
we organize but how loudly we howl

the shrieking owl – tell me – will these fish –
this school – bow before me as I kiss you

among the rock sculptures, atop the hill
up the breeze in the tall grass?

in the tall grass up the breeze
atop the mountain among the geodes

as I taste her, this land kneels before me
these swimmers swim in a trio

the shrieking owl – yowls – and speaks
this is the sensual revolution

I am Infamy and Bias – the night crawler
in your coffee cup the next morning

Enjoy these other titles by Andrew Garrison,
featuring a roster of talented and accomplished writers.

Available from Amazon.

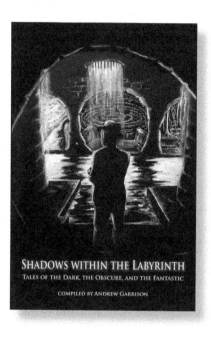

Shadows within the Labyrinth
*Tales of the Dark, the Obscure,
and the Fantastic*

featuring:
Andrew Cogburn
C. Vincent DeVellis
Andrew Garrison
A.C. Hernandez
Rosemary Jeffers
Benjamin Kissell
Michael Petrino Jr.
B.L. Rich
James R. Scrimgeour
Mick Theebs,
Jenna Anne Waltuch,
Christopher Wilbur

ISBN: 978-0-692-93081-6

America in Twilight
*Not Quite True Tales & Poems
through America*

featuring:
Michael Bentivegna
John Briggs,
C. Vincent DeVellis
Andrew Garrison
Lauren Kelly
Benjamin Kissell
Lou Orfanella
Michael Petrino, Jr.
James R. Scrimgeour
Mick Theebs

ISBN: 978-0-692-39604-9